MW00900422

IPHONE 14 PRO

AND PRO MAX

USER GUIDE

**The Complete Manual For Beginners
And Seniors With Instructions On How
To Master The New Apple iPhone 14
Pro & Pro Max. With Illustrations &
iOS 16 Tips & Tricks**

By

Alan McDonald

© Copyright 2022 Alan McDonald

All rights reserved. No part of this book shall be reproduced, stored in a retrieval system, or transmitted by any means, electronic, mechanical, photocopying, recording, or otherwise, without written permission from the publisher. Although every precaution has been taken in the preparation of this book, the publisher and author assume no responsibility for errors or omissions. Nor is any liability assumed for damages resulting from the use of the information contained herein.

Contents

INTRODUCTION

Both the iPhone 14 Pro and 14 Pro Max have a lot of new and better features. Here's everything you need to know about the new Pro models.

Apple has released the iPhone 14 series, and the iPhone 14 Pro and 14 Pro Max are the best phones this year. Like the iPhone 12 and iPhone 13 series, the iPhone 14 series comes in four different styles. But Apple stopped making the iPhone mini less than two years after it came out and put out the iPhone 14 Plus instead. The size of the new Plus model is the same as the iPhone 14 Pro Max, but it doesn't have as many high-end features.

This year, Apple seems to be making a change to its iPhones that will last. The iPhone 14 and iPhone 14 Plus have most of the same features as the iPhone 13. This means that they are sticking with the same A15 Bionic chipset and wide-notch design. The iPhone 14 Pro and Pro Max are the real successors of the iPhone 13 series since they have all the improvements.

DESIGN

Since the iPhone X came out in 2017, Apple has used the same big notch. The design hasn't changed in a long time, and it's time for a change. The notch on the iPhone 14 Pro model is the first to have a new look. Everyone was surprised when Apple showed off Dynamic Island, which is a big pill-shaped notch that hides the front camera and Faces ID sensors and also works as a notification bar. Dynamic Island could also grow to show users things going on in the background, like maps, music, and the timer.

The iPhone 14 Pro models look almost the same on the outside as the iPhone 13 Pro. They are made of stainless steel and have a screen protector called Ceramic Shield. Also, the IP68 rating has been kept, which means that the phone can stay dry for 30 minutes at a depth of up to six meters.

Apple has added a new Deep Purple color to the iPhone 14 Pro. Gold, Silver, and Space Black are the last three options. Alpine Green and Sierra Blue iPhone 13 Pro phones have been taken off the market, but Apple is likely to come out with a new color at some point.

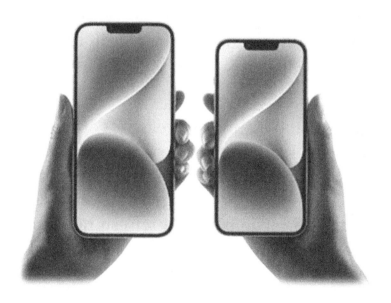

14 PRO MAX AND 14 PRO SPECIFICATION

Apple's newest processor, the A16 Bionic, is in the iPhone 14 Pro and Pro Max. Since the A16 is made with the same 5nm technology as the A15, the performance boost is not expected to be very big. Apple says that the six-core CPU in the A16 Bionic, which is made up of two performance cores and four efficiency cores, is 40 percent faster than the CPU in the A12 Bionic. It is said that the five-core GPU has 50 percent more memory bandwidth, which makes it better for gaming.

This means that the iPhone 13 Pro models still have the same amount of RAM. Still, there have been rumors in the past that Apple is switching to the faster LPDDR5 standard. Users will be able to choose between 128GB, 256GB, 512GB, and 1TB of storage.

The 6.1-inch and 6.7-inch screen sizes of the iPhone 14 Pro and 14 Pro Max are the same as those of their predecessors. The refresh rate is still 120Hz, but the Always-On display is a big improvement. The iPhone 14 Pro versions have a refresh rate that can go as low as 1Hz. This is something that Android phones have had for years. The current time, widgets, and Live Activities can now be shown on the lock screen. It even shows the wallpaper on the lock screen while reducing the number of colors to save power. The maximum brightness outside has been raised to 2,000 nits, which is another big change for the iPhone 14 Pro models.

Crash Detection and Satellite Emergency SOS are two new features that come with every iPhone 14.

With a new accelerometer and gyroscope, the iPhone 14 can now call 911 right away if you are in a car accident. The new Emergency SOS feature can talk directly to satellites, so users can call emergency services even when they don't have cellular or Wi-Fi service. The iPhone 14 can connect to a moving satellite to allow texting, and trained professionals will be able to call emergency services on behalf of the user. Starting in November, the function will only be available in the United States and Canada, and it will be free for two years.

As was already expected, Apple has taken the SIM card out of the new iPhones. This means that users will need eSIM to connect. Since eSIM is widely available from all of the major carriers, this shouldn't change how the user feels. eSIM is still a way for Apple to support dual-SIM functionality.

CHAPTER ONE

SET UP YOUR IPHONE

Before you can begin setting up your iPhone, you'll need the following items, whether you're switching from another phone or setting up your first iPhone:

Make a backup of your iPhone. If you're upgrading from an earlier iPhone, you'll be transferring data from your old phone to your new iPhone 14, so it's better to restore from a recent backup. If you lack sufficient storage space, you may back up to your PC.

Keep your old phone within reach. Whether it's an Android or an iPhone, you should have your prior phone available. This may speed up the installation procedure.

Additionally, bring your charger with you just in case. Even while the battery on your new iPhone 14 should be plenty to get you through the setup procedure, you may need to charge your older iPhone during the transfer.

Ensure that you can access the Internet. For iPhone setup, you must connect to a reliable Wi-Fi network.

Prepare your Apple ID credentials. Prepare your email address and password in case you need to check in to your Apple account to restore a backup or for other purposes. Additionally, you may make one during the setup process.

ACTIVATE YOUR IPHONE

Turning on your iPhone is the first step. Regardless of the model, turning it on is identical: Press and hold the side button on your iPhone's right side until the Apple logo appears. A few seconds should pass before the Hello screen appears. Swipe upward to start.

Follow the on-screen iPhone instructions

Now, you'll need to do a few small tasks on your iPhone to complete the initial setup, and happily, they're both simple. To begin, you will need to:

Choose a language: If you are in the United States, English should be listed first.

Choose your nation or area. Again, if you are in the United States, "United States" should appear at the top.

Use Quick Start to configure your iPhone.

On the next page, you will find the Quick Start screen, which enables you to automatically set up your iPhone 14 pro and iPhone 14 pro max using your previous iPhone or iPad. If you choose this method, you will need to power on your old device, connect it to Wi-Fi or cellular, and then bring it close to your new iPhone 14 pro and pro max.

You will then be prompted to authenticate or pair the two phones. You may use the camera on your old iPhone to scan the pattern on your new iPhone, or you may input a verification code. The activation process will take a few minutes.

Note: If you want to do these steps manually, go to the next section.

You will next be requested to do the following actions, among others:

Connect your Apple iPhone to your Wi-Fi network.

Set Up eSIM. You should see two options: Transfer from an existing iPhone (the preferred option) and Set Up Later under Settings. If you choose the first option, you will be prompted to double-press the side button on your previous iPhone.

Configure Face ID

Select how you would want to transmit your data. You may do it either using iCloud or your prior iPhone.

It is recommended to keep both devices connected to a power source throughout this process since it might take some time depending on the number of applications and the amount of data you have. Follow all the procedures until you have access to iOS 16 on your iPhone 14 pro and are done.

Configure your iPhone 14 pro and iPhone 14 pro max manually

Tap Set Up Manually on the Quick Start screen if you are switching from an Android phone or another phone, or if you want to set up your iPhone manually. If you choose this path, you will need to manually complete the following tasks:

Access a Wi-Fi network. Wait a few minutes for the activation of your phone.

Read the prompt for Data & Privacy. Once you are completed, click Continue.

Prepare to Face This is how the iPhone 14 pro max will be unlocked using face recognition.

To get into your iPhone 14pro and pro max, make a six-digit passcode. This is your back-up plan for unlocking your iPhone 14. Type in the passcode twice.

Select the method for restoring your applications and data. You can restore from an iCloud backup, a Mac or PC, transfer directly from an iPhone, transfer data from an Android device, or choose not to transfer applications and data.

- Depending on how you choose to restore your apps and data, you may need to use your iCloud credentials to sign in to your Apple account. Then, you must enter a verification code that may show up on one of your other devices to prove that you are who you say you are.
- Next, accept the terms and conditions, change your preferences, update to the latest version of iOS, and set up Apple Pay, Siri, and Screen Time if you need to.
- Last, set up the True Tone display, choose the light or dark mode, and decide whether you want a normal view or a zoomed view (for those that have impaired vision).

iOS 16 is now compatible with iPhone 14 PRO and PRO MAX

When you're done, you can swipe up to get into your iPhone. You might not see all of your apps on your home screen or all of your photos and videos in your camera roll, so you will need to be patient while your iPhone 14 uploads all of your apps and data. This could take several hours, depending on how much money needs to be sent.

SIGN IN TO YOUR ICLOUD

Sign in to all of your devices using the same Apple ID and password to set up iCloud. You may pick independently on each device which applications store information in iCloud and whatever iCloud capabilities you use.

When iCloud is turned off for an app or feature on a device, the information saved in iCloud for that app or feature is no longer available on that device. However, it remains accessible on other devices when iCloud is enabled for the app or functionality in question.

CONFIGURE ICLOUD ON YOUR IOS DEVICE

Navigate to Settings > [your name] on your iPhone.

If your name is not shown, touch "Sign in to your device" and enter your Apple ID and password.

Perform one of the subsequent:

iOS 16: Tap iCloud, then enable each desired app or functionality. Tap Show All to see other applications.

CHAPTER TWO

IOS 16 NEW FEATURES

LOCK DISPLAY

Lock Gallery display

For ideas on how to personalize the Lock Screen, peruse a gallery of alternatives, each with a distinctive background, stylized depiction of the date and time, and quick-view information.

Lock Screen toggle

The Lock Screen may be changed during the day. Touch and hold it before swiping.

prevent screen editing

By touching the element, it's simple to change the font, color, or positioning of components on the Lock Screen.

Formatted date and time

You may alter the appearance of the date and time on your Lock Screen using a variety of font styles and colors.

layered photographic effect

The picture topic is dynamically displayed in front of the time to make it stand out.

Recommended photographs

iOS automatically recommends images from your picture collection that would look fantastic on the Lock Screen.

Image shuffle

View a randomized collection of photographs on your Lock Screen. Set the frequency with which your Lock Screen receives a new picture, or let iOS surprise and amuse you throughout the day.

Photo styles

You can give photos on the Lock Screen styles that automatically change the color filter, tint, and text style to match.

There are widgets on the Lock Screen.

You can choose to put a group of widgets on your Lock Screen to give you quick access to things like the weather, time, date, battery level, upcoming calendar events, alarms, time zones, and the progress of your Activity ring.

WidgetKit API

Check out widgets from the third-party apps you like. Close to the time, you can look at widgets that are text-based, circular, or rectangular to see things like the weather or your goal progress.

Actual Activities

Live Activities let you keep up with what's going on in real-time right from your Lock Screen.

API for Live Activities

With just a glance, you can see how a game, your ride, or your order is going. With the help of the new developer API, you may be able to see Live Activities from your favorite third-party apps.

Lock Screens for Concentration

iOS has a set of Lock Screens that go with the different Focus options. For example, the Work Focus has a Lock Screen with a lot of information, while the Personal Focus has a picture Lock Screen.

Apple collections

Choose from several Lock Screens made just for iOS 16 that are dynamic, classic, or landscape. There are Lock Screens in Apple's collections that honor cultural events like Pride and Unity.

Astronomy

You can look at the earth, moon, and solar system with a set of Lock Screens based on astronomy that change based on what's going on in real-time.

Weather

Watch the weather in real-time on your Lock Screen as the day goes on.

Emoji

Make patterns for your Lock Screen that look like your favorite emoji.

Colors

Choose a color gradient for your Lock Screen with the colors you like best.

Novel notification layout

The combination of strong text and photos helps alerts visually stand out.

Animations for notifications

Now, your notifications, including a summary of them, will show up at the bottom of your Lock Screen. This makes it easier to see them as they come in.

Notification view when Locked

To show alerts on the Lock Screen, you can choose between an extended list view, a stacking view, or a count view. You can pinch to change the layout of the context.

FOCUS

Lock Screen connecting

By connecting your Lock Screen to your Focus, you will change both the way your iPhone looks and how it works. If you swipe to the Focus's Lock Screen, you can turn it on.

Lock Screen recommendations

iOS has a set of Lock Screens that go with the different Focus options. For example, the Work Focus has a Lock Screen with a lot of information, while the Personal Focus has a picture Lock Screen.

Suggestions for the Homepage page

iOS suggests Home Screen pages with apps and widgets that are most useful for the Focus you are setting up.

Contrast filters

You can set limits in Apple apps like Calendar, Mail, Messages, and Safari for each Focus that is turned on. You can choose which Tab Groups to show in Safari when you're in the Work Focus, for example, or hide your work calendar when you're in the Personal Focus.

API for focus filter

With the new Focus filter API, developers can hide things that are distracting by using the signal you send to turn on Focus.

Focus agendas

Set a Focus to turn on automatically at a certain time or place, or when you use a certain app.

Easier setup

Start using Focus by following a setup process that is different for each option.

Allow and suppress the list

When setting up a Focus, you can choose which apps and contacts you want to get alerts from by turning them on or off.

Apple's iCloud Shared Photo Library

Share a group of pictures with your family.

Share a different set of photos in iCloud with up to five other people.

Smart setup rules

You can share all of your historical images or use the setup tools to choose which images to share based on when they were taken or who they are off.

Brilliant sharing tips

You can manually share photos or use smart features like a switch in the Camera, Bluetooth proximity-based automatic sharing, and sharing recommendations in For You to make sharing easy.

Cooperate on the compilation

All users have the same rights to add, edit, favorite, caption, and delete.

Relive more full recollections

Through Memories, Featured Photos, and the Photos widget, you can look at pictures that other people have shared.

MESSAGES

Edit a message

After you send a message, you have 15 minutes to change it. Recipients will be able to see a log of all the changes made to a message.

Undo send

Within two minutes of sending a message, you can send it again.

Mark as not read.

Mark messages as unread if you don't have time to respond but want to remember to reply later.

Get back some lost messages

You can get back deleted messages for up to 30 days after you delete them.

SharePlay by sending a message

Share synchronized activities like movies, music, exercises, games, and more while talking to friends through Messages.

You shared API with

When someone sends you a video or article that you don't have time to look at right away, it will be easy to find when you open the app again.

Collaboration requests

If you use Messages to invite people to work together on a document, spreadsheet, or project, everyone on the thread will be added to the document, spreadsheet, or project right away. It works with Files, Keynote, Numbers, Pages, Notes, Reminders, Safari, and applications from other companies.

Collaboration moves forward

Activity updates will be shown at the top of the Messages thread when someone makes a change. Tap on the changes to go back to the group project.

API for Working Together on Messages

Developers can connect their app's collaboration features to Messages and FaceTime. This makes it easy to start and manage collaboration right from the places where people are already talking.

Text Messages in Threads

When an iOS user answers a text message in an SMS thread with a tap back, their answer shows up in the bubble for that message in Messages.

Dual SIM message filtering

In Messages, you can filter chats by SIM.

Reproducing an audio message

You can move audio messages forward or backward as you listen.

MAIL

Smart search corrections

Intelligent search improves the results by fixing misspelled words and using similar words for search terms.

Smart search suggestions

When you start looking for email messages, you'll see more shared content and other things.

Leaving out the recipient and the attachment

Get a reminder if you forget to add something important, like an attachment or a recipient, to your message.

Undo send

You can easily stop an email from going to the recipient's inbox before it gets there.

transmission planned

Plan to send emails at the best times.

Follow-up

Move the emails you've sent to the top of your inbox so you can quickly reply.

Remind me

Don't forget about an email you opened but didn't answer. Choose when you want messages to come back to your inbox.

Rich link

Add links to your emails that give a quick overview of the situation and more information.

BIMI support

With BIMI (Brand Indicators for Message Identification)-verified brand iconography, it's easy to tell when an email is from an authorized source.

SAFARI

Collective Tab Groups

Share tabs with your friends. Everyone can add their tabs and quickly watch the Tab Group change as they collaborate.

Tab Group beginning pages

You may personalize Tab Group start pages with a background picture and your preferences.

Tabs pinned inside Tab Groups

Customize Tab Groups by pinning certain tabs to each group.

New APIs for web extension

Allows developers to build more types of Safari extensions.

Internet push notifications

Added support for optin iOS notifications. Arriving in 2023

Extensions synchronization

In Safari's options, you can see which extensions are available on your other devices. Once an extension is installed, it syncs so that you only have to turn it on once.

Settings for websites are synced. Settings for some websites, like page zoom and automatic Reader view, are the same on all devices.

New languages

Safari can now translate web pages into Arabic, Dutch, Indonesian, Korean, Polish, Thai, Turkish, and Vietnamese.

Website images in other languages

Live Text can now translate text that is in a photo.

Help for other technologies on the web

Gives developers more power and control over the design and layout of web pages, which makes it easier for them to make more interesting content.

Strong password management

Change the strong passwords Safari suggests to fit the needs of a specific site.

Wi-Fi passwords in Settings

You can find and change your Wi-Fi passwords in the Settings menu. Refer to and trade passwords, or delete passwords that aren't being used.

Passkeys

Passkeys

Passkeys are a simpler and more secure way to log in than using a password.

Safe from phishing

Passkeys don't leave your device and are only used on the website you made them for. This makes it almost impossible to use them for phishing.

Protect your website from hackers.

Your private key is never saved on a web server, so website leaks can't give hackers access to your accounts.

Sign in on more gadgets

Face ID lets you use your iPhone or iPad to scan a QR code and sign in to websites or apps on other devices, even ones that aren't Apple.

synchronize devices

Passkeys are secured end-to-end and synchronized across all of your Apple devices using iCloud Keychain.

ACTUAL TEXT

Real-Time Text in video

Text in stopped video frames is fully interactive, allowing you to perform capabilities like copy and paste, lookup, and translate. Live Text operates in Photos, Quick Look, Safari, and other applications.

Move quickly

With a simple swipe, you can get to photos and movies that have data that can be used. You can track planes or shipments, translate languages, and do a lot more with GPS.

Languages that Live Text now supports

Text written in Japanese, Korean, and Ukrainian can now be read by Live Text.

SIRI

Set up simple short cuts

Siri can run app shortcuts without having to be set up.

Send messages out automatically.

When sending a message, the confirmation step is skipped. This feature can be turned on in Settings.

Emoji in texts

Siri can send messages that include emojis.

Siri, what can I do here?

"Hey Siri, what can I do here?" is a good way to find out what Siri's iOS and apps can do.

"You can also ask Siri about an app by saying something like, "Hey Siri, what can I do with iRobot?"

Call hang up

Siri can end a call for you without you having to use your hands. Just say "Hey Siri, hang up" (participants on the call will hear you). This feature can be turned on in Settings.

Better help when you're not online

Siri can answer questions about Home Control (HomeKit), Intercom, and Voicemail even when it's not connected to the internet.

Dictation

Dictation experience with new ideas

When dictating on a device, you can switch between speech and touch without any trouble. You can type with the keyboard, tap in the text field, move the cursor, and use QuickType suggestions without stopping Dictation.

Auto-punctuation

Dictation will add commas, periods, and question marks for you as you talk.

Emoji support

When using your voice to dictate on a device, you can add emojis.

Dictation in the field for Messages

In the text field of Messages, there is now an icon for Dictation.

Muffin dictation

Tap the new pop-up cursor to stop Dictation right away.

MAPS

Route with multiple stops

Maps lets you add many stops along your route. If you plan a trip with more than one stop on your Mac, it will sync to your iPhone.

Maps transit cards

You can add transportation cards to your Wallet, check to see if they have low balances and reload them without leaving Maps.

Transit fares

Use transportation fares to figure out how much your trip will cost.

PAY WITH APPLE AND A WALLET

Apple Payments came later.

You can pay for an Apple Pay Later purchase in four interest-free payments over six weeks.

Key exchange

Use your favorite messaging app, like Messages, Mail, or WhatsApp, to send your Apple Wallet keys to people you trust.

Applications showed ID cards

Share your ID information with apps that need to check your age and identity. Apps will only ask for the information they need to complete a transaction. You will be able to look over this request, but your information won't be given out until Face ID or Touch ID has been used to prove who you are.

Cash center every day

As part of Apple Card, the Daily Cash portal lets you learn how to earn Daily Cash, check how much Daily Cash you've earned so far, track your progress toward offers, and find the most recent Bonus Daily Cash Merchants.

Apple Cash

Wallet's Apple Cash payment requests make it easier to manage active payment requests from your Apple Cash card.

Verification of identity in applications

Customers in the United States will be able to share the verified information on their ID cards with apps that need to check their age or identity.

Multi-stay hotel keys

You don't have to add a new hotel key to your Wallet every time you make a new reservation. When you stay at hotels of the same brand in the future, you only need one key to check in and get into your room.

Add keys from Safari

You can now add extra keys to your iPhone and Apple Watch without having to download an app. You can do this right from a webpage in Safari.

Easy to move key devices

Tap the "+" button in Wallet to see a list of all your keys and choose the ones you want to add to the new device.

Taking care of Apple Pay orders

Apple Pay Order Tracking lets people get full receipts and information about where their orders are in Wallet for Apple Pay purchases made at participating stores.

Tokens for stores that accept Apple Pay

Merchant Tokens make it possible to set up and run recurring or pre-approved Apple Pay payments safely.

With Apple Pay, you can pay more than one store at the same time.

You can now enter purchase amounts for more than one store on a single Apple Pay payment sheet. This lets you buy a package deal, such as a flight, rental car, and hotel for a vacation, and then transfer payments to different merchants.

Easy-to-use menu

The fast access menu, which is available on some passes and cards, lets users access different back-pass functions with just one press.

Improve your Apple account

Using the card stored in Wallet, a customer can add money to their Apple Account.

Home

Categories

The "Lights," "Temperature," "Security," "Speakers and TVs," and "Water" categories make it easy to find all the accessories you need, organized by room, as well as information about their status.

New point of view

On the Home page, up to four camera views are shown prominently, and you can easily scroll to see more.

Tile design

The accessory tiles have been changed so that you can tell the different kinds of accessories apart by their shape and color. You can control accessories right from their tiles by touching the icon, or you can get to more controls by touching the name of the accessory.

Added new features to buildings

Because the underlying architecture has been improved, smart homes with a lot of smart accessories work faster and are more reliable. Using the Home app, you can talk to and control connected devices from different devices at once.

On the Lock Screen, there are widgets.

With the new widgets on the iPhone Lock Screen, you can see how your home is doing and get to your favorite accessories right from the Lock Screen.

Matter support

The matter is a new way for smart home devices to connect. It will allow devices from different platforms to work together. The matter will give you access to even more smart home accessories that work with the Home app and Siri on iOS devices.

HEALTH

Monitor your prescriptions

Create a list of your prescriptions, vitamins, and supplements to keep track of them. And add personalized images to make them easier to recall.

Add meds using the camera on your iPhone

You may simply add your prescriptions using the camera on your iPhone. Simply place the medication's label in the frame, and the medication's name, strength, and dosage form will be shown.

Reminders about drugs

Whether you take prescriptions numerous times a day, once a week, or as required, create individual schedules and reminders for each drug.

Medication logging

Record when you have taken your drugs using a reminder or directly in the Health app. Charts that are interactive assist you comprehend when you've taken your meds and provide insight into your adherence.

Learn more about the drugs you take

This includes how to pronounce the name, what the drug is used for, how the medication functions, and probable adverse effects.

Drug-drug interactions

Combining some drugs might reduce their efficacy or induce unwanted side effects. When you add a new drug, you will get a warning if there is a serious interaction. In the Health app, you may examine critical, severe, and moderate encounters.

Requests for Health Care Sharing

Invite your loved ones to confidentially share their medical information with you. After receiving your invitation, they may pick which information to give.

Cycle deviation notice

If your recorded menstrual cycles reveal a trend of infrequent periods, irregular periods, longer periods, or chronic spotting, you might get a notice.

FITNESS

Fitness application for all iOS users

Even without an Apple Watch, you can track and fulfill your exercise goals. Using the motion sensors on your iPhone, your steps, distance, and third-party exercises will provide an estimate of the calories that will contribute to your daily Move target.

Sharing Among Families

Improved setup of child accounts

Set up a child's account from the start with the necessary parental controls, including simple, age-appropriate recommendations for media limitations.

Device setup for kids

Using Quick Start, you can quickly configure a new iOS or iPadOS device for your kid with all the necessary parental settings already enabled.

Requests for Screen Time in Messages

Requests for Screen Time from your children now display in Messages, making it simple to accept or deny a request.

Household Checklist

Family Checklist provides useful recommendations and ideas, such as updating a child's preferences as they age, enabling location sharing, and reminding you that your iCloud+ membership may be shared with everyone.

CARPLAY

Generation succeeding CarPlay

The newest edition of CarPlay integrates the driver's experience across all displays. Deep connectivity with the vehicle's systems enables the instrument cluster to show driving information and to manage the radio and climate system. This latest version of CarPlay is tailored to each vehicle's screen size, shape, and layout. New degrees of customization enables drivers to customize the style of their instrument cluster, including brand-specific choices.

Fueling and driving task applications

CarPlay offers applications for fueling and driving-related tasks. CarPlay can accommodate your favorite applications that help you refuel and give route information, toll support, and towing assistance, among others.

Automatically transmit communications

The confirmation step is skipped while sending messages. Under CarPlay, you may activate this option in Siri's settings.

PRIVACY

Security Check

This new feature in Settings allows victims of domestic or intimate partner abuse to rapidly revoke the permissions they've given others. It also allows you to regulate access granted to individuals and applications.

Pasteboard authorization

Apps require your permission to use the clipboard to copy and paste material from another app.

Streaming media enhancements

Stream video directly from devices that support protocols other than AirPlay without providing Bluetooth or local network access authorization.

Lock Photos' Hidden and Recently Deleted albums

The Hidden and Recently Deleted albums are by default protected and may be opened using Face ID or a password.

SECURITY

Fast Security Steps

You can get important security updates for your devices even faster. Between regular software updates, these changes can be made automatically.

Panorama Face ID is a way to tell who you are.

On iPhones that can use Face ID, it works in landscape mode.

Put on the brakes

This new security mode gives the highest level of protection to the small number of people whose digital security is at risk from severe, targeted threats. It makes your device even more secure and severely limits some of its capabilities. This makes it much harder for highly targeted mercenary malware to attack your device.

ACCESSIBILITY

The Apple Watch shows

To get the most out of your Apple Watch, use Switch Control, Voice Control, and any other helper features on your iPhone.

Mode of Detection in a Magnifier

With the new Magnifier mode, which includes Door Detection, People Detection, and Image Explanations, you can get detailed descriptions of what's going on around you.

Using a magnifying glass to find doors

Find a door, look at any labels or signs near it, and find out how to open it.

Buddy controller

By putting the inputs from multiple game controllers into one, your caretaker or friend will be able to help you get to the next level of your game.

Siri call hang up

Siri can end a call for you without you having to use your hands. Just say "Hey Siri, hang up" (participants on the call will hear you). This feature can be turned on in Settings.

Voice Control call disconnect

You can now end Phone and FaceTime calls with your voice. To end a call, just say "end call" when Voice Control is on (participants on the call will hear you).

Captions

Users who are deaf or hard of hearing can get automatic, real-time transcriptions so they can follow conversations, audio, and video more easily.

Adding captions to FaceTime

Add speech recognition to your FaceTime video chats. With speaker ID, it's easy to keep up with group chats.

Books now have new features to make them easier to use.

There are new themes and ways to change things, like making text bold, changing lines, characters, word spacing, and more.

VoiceOver and spoken content will have more voices and languages.

VoiceOver and Spoken Content are now available in more than twenty new languages and regions, such as Bangla (India), Bulgarian, Catalan, Ukrainian, and Vietnamese. Also, you can choose from hundreds of other voices that are good for assistive features.

Hearing aids should be able to get alerts from Siri.

Using Siri, you can have hearing aids made for iPhone and send out iPhone alerts.

Siri pause time

Set how long Siri should wait for you to finish talking before responding.

Siri lets you turn on and turn off auto-answer for calls

Siri can turn auto-answer on or off for Phone and FaceTime calls.

VoiceOver lets you know where you are in Maps.

VoiceOver users will now automatically hear and feel a beep and vibration when walking directions start in Maps.

Voice Control spelling mode

The Spelling mode of Voice Control lets you spell names, addresses, and other words in your way.

Functions of the Magnifier

You can save your favorite settings for the Magnifier, like camera, brightness, contrast, and filters, for activities and situations that you do often.

Add a recording of sound to Health.

Bring your audiograms into the Health app on your iPhone.

More options for customizing sound recognition

You can teach your iPhone to listen to sounds that are only found in your area, like the beep of a kitchen appliance or the exact sound of your doorbell.

USE SIRI ON IPHONE

Use just your voice to do common chores. Use Siri to translate a sentence, set an alarm, locate a place, and get a weather report, among other things.

On compatible devices, voice input is handled by iPhone, but Apple receives a transcript of your requests to enhance Siri. This information is not linked to your Apple ID, and it will only be kept for a short time. You can also choose to let Siri and Dictation get better. If you agree, Apple will share the audio of your interactions with Siri, Dictation, and Translate to help develop and improve Siri, Dictation, and other languages processing features like Translate or Voice Control.

For some things, the iPhone needs to be connected to the internet. There may be fees for cell phones.

HOW TO SET UP SIRI

If you didn't set up Siri when you first set up your iPhone, go to Settings > Siri & Search and then do one of the following:

If you want to talk to Siri to turn it on: Enable Listening for "Hey Siri"

- Turn on Siri by pressing the side button (on an iPhone with Face ID)

ACTIVATE SIRI VIA SPOKEN COMMAND

When Siri is activated by speech, Siri answers verbally.

Say "Hey Siri" followed by your query or request.

For example, say "Hey Siri, what's the weather forecast for today?" or "Hey Siri, set an alarm for eight in the morning."

To ask other questions or make additional requests, repeat "Hey Siri" or press the Listen button.

Note: To prevent the iPhone from responding to "Hey Siri," put the device face down or go to Settings > Siri & Search and disable Siri. Listen for "Hey Siri."

Additionally, you can activate Siri by saying "Hey Siri" when wearing supporting AirPods.

ACTIVATE SIRI BY PRESSING A BUTTON

When Siri is activated with a button when the iPhone is in quiet mode, Siri answers silently. When the quiet mode is off, Siri speaks out loud.

Perform one of the subsequent:

- On an iPhone equipped with Face ID, hold down the side button.

Ask Siri a question or make a request when she emerges.

For instance, you can ask, "What is 18 percent of 225?" Set the timer for three minutes.

To submit an additional question or request, touch the Listen button.

On compatible AirPods, you may also activate Siri by touching the earbud. Consult Siri Setup in the AirPods User Guide.

CORRECT SIRI IF SHE MISUNDERSTANDS YOU.

Rephrase your request: Tap "Listen," and then say your question again.

Spell out part of your request: Tap the Listen button, and then spell out any words Siri didn't know. For example, you could say "Call" and then the person's name.

Change a message before sending it: Say "Change it."

If your request shows up on the screen, you can add words to change it. Touch the request, and then use the on-screen keyboard.

TYPE RATHER THAN SPEAKING TO SIRI

- Navigate to Settings > Accessibility > Siri and enable Type to Siri.
- Siri must be activated before a question or request can be typed using the keyboard and text field.

- iPhone's Siri can announce calls, texts, and other information.

Siri can announce incoming calls and alerts from applications like Messages over compatible headphones and CarPlay. You may respond with your voice without first saying "Hey Siri."

Announce Calls and Announce Notifications are also compatible with third-party applications.

HAVE SIRI ANNOUNCE CALLS

With Announce Calls, Siri announces incoming phone calls and FaceTime calls, allowing you to verbally accept or refuse them.

- Choose an option from Settings > Siri & Search > Announce Calls.

When a call comes in, Siri sees who is calling and asks if you want to take it. Choose "yes" if you want to take the call or "no" if you don't.

HAVE SIRI ANNOUNCE ALERTS

Siri can broadcast upcoming alerts from applications like Messages and Reminders. Siri will turn on app notifications automatically for time-sensitive apps, but you can always change the settings. Visit the link to learn more about alerts that must be dealt with quickly.

- Go to Settings > Siri & Search > Announce Notifications to turn on Announce Notifications.
- Tap the app for which you'd want Siri to announce alerts, then tap Announce Notifications.

You may choose whether to broadcast all notifications or just time-sensitive ones for certain applications.

For reply-enabled applications, like Apple Messages, Siri repeats what you said, then requests confirmation before delivering your reply. Enable Reply Without Confirmation to send responses without waiting for confirmation.

CHANGE IPHONE SIRI SETTINGS

You may alter Siri's voice and limit access to Siri while your smartphone is locked.

CHANGE SIRI'S RESPONSE TIME

Siri may be configured to react to voice commands or button presses. You may also choose the language in which Siri answers.

Go to Settings > Siri & Search, and then do one of the following:

Stop Siri from responding when you say "Hey Siri": Turn off Siri. Wait for "Hey Siri."

Stop Siri from responding when you press the side or Home button: Turn off (on an iPhone with Face ID) Press Side Button for Siri or Press Home for Siri (on an iPhone with a Home button).

Prevent Siri access while the iPhone is locked: Disable Allow Siri While Locked.

Change Siri's language of response: Select a new language by tapping Language.

SIRI MAY ALSO BE ACTIVATED BY TYPING.

- Change Siri's vocalization
- You may alter Siri's voice (not available for all languages).
- Navigate to Settings > Siri & Search menu.
- Tap Siri Voice, then choose a different voice variation.

MODIFY SIRI'S RESPONSES

Siri may answer audibly or in silence (with text onscreen). Your request is also shown onscreen.

Navigate to Settings > Siri & Search, and then do one of the following:

Change Siri's voice response behavior: Tap Siri Responses, then choose an option from the list under Spoken Responses.

Always see Siri's responses on-screen: Tap Siri Responses, and then toggle Always Display Siri Captions.

See your request onscreen: Tap Siri Responses, then toggle Always Display Speech.

USE AND PERSONALIZE IPHONE'S CONTROL CENTER

The iPhone's Control Center provides quick access to important features and applications, including airplane mode, Do Not Disturb, a flashlight, volume, and screen brightness.

OPEN CONTROL CENTER

On an iPhone equipped with Face ID, swipe down from the upper-right corner. Swipe upwards from the bottom to dismiss Control Center.

Swipe up from the bottom on an iPhone with a Home button. Swipe down or hit the Home button to exit Control Center.

ACCESS MORE CONTROL CENTER CONTROLS

Touch and hold to see Camera options.

Numerous controls give supplementary choices. To see the choices available, touch and hold control. Control Center allows you to conduct the following, for instance:

- Touch and hold the set of controls in the upper-left corner, then press the AirDrop button to access the AirDrop choices.
- Touch and hold the Camera button to capture a selfie, photograph, or video.

ADD AND ARRANGE CONTROL BUTTONS
You can change Control Center by adding more controls and shortcuts to different apps like Calculator, Notes, Voice Memos, and more.

- Go to Configuration > Control Center.
- Press Insert or the label of the control you want to add or remove.
- To move a control, touch the Reorder button next to it and then drag it to a new spot.

DISCONNECT FROM A WI-FI NETWORK TEMPORARILY.
- To get back online, press the Wi-Fi Switch button in Control Center again.
- Press and hold the Wi-Fi Switch button to see the name of the connected Wi-Fi network.

Because Wi-Fi doesn't turn off when you leave a network, AirPlay and AirDrop still work, and when you move or restart your iPhone, it automatically connects to known networks. To disable Wi-Fi, go to Settings > Wi-Fi. To turn on Wi-Fi again, tap the Wi-Fi Switch button in Control Center. Find out how to use Control Center while in airplane mode to turn on or off Wi-Fi.

DISCONNECT TEMPORARILY FROM BLUETOOTH DEVICES

Double-tap the Bluetooth Switch button in Control Center to turn on Bluetooth connections.

Because Bluetooth doesn't turn off when you disconnect from a device, location services, and other services still work. To turn Bluetooth off, go to Settings > Bluetooth, and then turn Bluetooth off. To turn Bluetooth back on, tap the Bluetooth Switch button in Control Center. Find out how to turn Bluetooth on or off in Control Center when you are in airplane mode.

Disable Control Center access in applications

Navigate to Settings > Control Center and disable Access Within Apps.

CHAPTER THREE

NOTIFICATION AND ALERTS

Learn how to access and modify notification settings and enable or disable alerts.

View notifications

To see recent notifications, use the Notification Center by swiping down from the top of the screen.

ACCESS AND MODIFY NOTIFICATION SETTINGS

To access the settings for notifications, click the settings app from the home screen.

Select Notifications, then modify the required settings.

CUSTOMIZE ALERTS PER APPLICATION

To modify the notification settings for a specific app, choose the app in question. Change the settings for notifications as desired. To enable or disable app notifications, toggle the Allow Notifications option.

To modify the particular app's Sound notifications, pick Sounds and then the appropriate choice.

To activate or disable app badges, use the Badges on/off switch.

CHANGE THE DO NOT DISTURB SETTING.

To rapidly toggle Do Not Disturb on or off, open the Control Center by swiping down from the top right corner of the screen, then selecting Focus > Do Not Disturb. When Do Not Disturb is activated, all incoming calls and alerts are muted.

- To modify Do Not Disturb settings, choose Focus > Do Not Disturb > Edit Settings from the Settings menu.
- When Do Not Disturb is activated, the Lock screen will show a dnd Do Not Disturb symbol.

CHANGE GOVERNMENT ALERT SETTINGS

Select Notifications and then GOVERNMENT ALERTS from the Settings menu. To turn notifications on or off, choose the button next to the selected government alert.

Select an alert grouping

Select Notification Grouping from the Notifications settings page of the relevant application. After selecting the desired option, choose the back arrow.

CUSTOMIZE THE IPHONE LOCK SCREEN

You can change your Lock Screen in a lot of ways, such as by adding wallpaper, changing the colors and fonts, putting images over the clock, and a lot more. You can also add widgets to your Lock Screen that show information from your favorite apps, like the news for today, the weather, and upcoming calendar events.

You can set up a lot of different Lock Screens and switch between them. Since each Lock Screen can be linked to a different Focus, you can change your Focus by choosing a different Lock Screen.

- Face ID makes it easy to build a customized Lock Screen

CREATE A PERSONALIZED LOCK SCREEN

Touch and hold the Lock Screen until the button that says "Customize" shows up.

- If you don't see the Customize button, tap and hold the Lock Screen again, and then enter your passcode.

- Choose the "Add New" button at the bottom of the screen.
- The wallpaper collection for the Lock Screen displays.
- Tap a picture to make it the background of your Lock Screen.

For some wallpaper options, you can swipe left or right to try out different color filters, patterns, and fonts that go well together.

Tap Add, then follow one of the steps below:

Select whether the wallpaper should be used on both the Lock Screen and Home Screen: Tap Set as Background Pair.

Make more changes to the Home Screen: Tap Customize Home Screen. You can change the color of the wallpaper by tapping a color, tapping the Photo On Rectangle button to use a custom image, or tapping Blur to make the background blurry and draw attention to the apps.

ADD AN IMAGE TO THE LOCK SCREEN

You can add a picture to your Lock Screen by choosing one from your photo library or by letting your iPhone suggest a picture that goes well with the other settings you have for your Lock Screen.

- Touch and hold the Lock Screen until the button that says "Customize" shows up.
- If you don't see the Customize button, tap and hold the Lock Screen again, and then enter your passcode.
- Tap the "Add" button at the bottom of the screen. Then, at the top of the screen, choose either "Photos" or "Photo Shuffle."
- If you choose Photos and want to make an effect with multiple layers, choose More and then Depth Effect.

This feature might not work with all images. Backgrounds with widgets can't be put on top of each other. Models that can be built can use the multilayered effect. Layering is only possible with photos that have people, animals, or the sky in them, but not with all photos in those categories. Layering might not be possible if the topic is too high, too low, or covers too much of the clock.

To move a picture, pinch it open to zoom in, drag it with two fingers to where you want it, and then pinch it closed to zoom out.

You can also swipe left or right to try out different picture styles, such as color filters and fonts that go well together.

If you choose Photo Shuffle, you can see a preview of the photos by tapping the Browse button, and you can change how often the photos change by tapping the More button and choosing a different option from the drop-down menu under Shuffle Frequency.

You can put a picture from your photo library on the Home Screen and Lock Screen if you want to. Choose a picture from the Library in the Photos app, then tap the Share button. Choose Use as Wallpaper, tap Done, and then decide if you want the picture to show up on the Home Screen or the Lock Screen.

INCLUDE WIDGETS ON THE LOCK SCREEN
You can add widgets to your Lock Screen to get information quickly, like the current temperature, how much battery life you have left, and upcoming calendar events.

- Touch and hold the Lock Screen until the Customize button appears at the bottom of the screen, then touch Customize.
- If you don't see the Customize button, tap and hold the Lock Screen again, and then enter your passcode.

- To add widgets to your Lock Screen, tap Customize and then tap the box under the clock.
- Tap or move the widgets you want to add to add them.
- If you don't have enough room for a new widget, you can use the Remove Widget button to get rid of an existing widget and make room for a new widget.

On the iPhone 14 Pro and iPhone 14 Pro Max, you can set the Lock Screen to stay on so that you can always see the date, time, and widgets.

ALTERNATIVE LOCK SCREENS

You can make more than one Lock Screen and switch between them during the day. If a certain Focus is tied to a Lock Screen, switching from that Lock Screen to another Lock Screen will also change your Focus.

- Touch and hold the Lock Screen until the button that says "Customize" shows up.
- If you don't see the Customize button, tap and hold the Lock Screen again, and then enter your passcode.
- Swipe to the Lock Screen you want, then tap it.

MODIFY THE LOCK SCREEN

After you've made a custom Lock Screen, you can change it.

- Touch and hold the Lock Screen until the button that says "Customize" shows up.
- If you don't see the Customize button, tap and hold the Lock Screen again, and then enter your passcode.
- Swipe to the Lock Screen you want, and then tap the Add New button.

Perform any of the subsequent:

Select a wallpaper: Tap a category (like Featured, Suggested Photos, or Photo Shuffle) or a button at the top of the screen (Photos, People, Photo Shuffle, Emoji, or Weather). Follow these steps to add a picture to your Lock Screen.

Tap the box under the clock, and then tap the widgets you want to add.

Choose a picture style for a Lock Screen with a photograph: Swipe to change the color filter (like Vibrant, Tone, Deep, and Vapor), the picture background (Natural, Black & White, Duotone, and so on), and the time font.

Add a layered effect to a photo-based Lock Screen: Tap the More button in the bottom right corner, then choose Depth Effect (not available for all photos).

- Tap the Focus button at the bottom of the wallpaper, and then choose a different Focus from the menu that appears.
- Click Customize, touch the time, and then click the Custom Color button to change how the time looks.

In Settings, you can also add new background.

DELETE A LOCK SCREEN

You can get rid of Lock Screens that you don't need anymore.

- Touch and hold the Lock Screen until the button that says "Customize" shows up.
- If you don't see the Customize button, tap and hold the Lock Screen again, and then enter your passcode.

Swipe to the Lock Screen you want, swipe up and then press the Trash button.

CHAPTER FOUR

HOW TO CHANGE THE BACKGROUND IMAGE

Want to change your iPhone's wallpaper? You may choose a recommended background image or one of your photographs.

CHANGE YOUR LOCK SCREEN OR HOME SCREEN BACKGROUND

In the Settings application, choose Wallpaper.

- Tap Add a New Background.
- To pick your picture, choose Photos, People, or Photo Shuffle. Additionally, you may pick a wallpaper from categories such as Weather & Astronomy, Emoji, Collections, or Color.
- You may further personalize your background if you choose. Tap then Add.

LOCK SCREEN BACKGROUND CUSTOMIZATION

- Ensure that Face ID has been previously set up on your iPhone. Face ID must detect your eyes and surrounding regions to change your wallpaper from the Lock Screen.
- Touch and hold the Lock Screen to access your wallpaper gallery from the Lock Screen.
- To pick a previously made wallpaper, swipe left and right. To add a new desktop background, hit the Add button.
- You may also hit the Focus button from the Lock Screen wallpaper choices to associate a Focus with a particular wallpaper, tweak

existing wallpapers, or swipe up on the wallpaper and tap to remove it.

- If you can't change the Lock Screen with Face ID, tap and hold the Lock Screen until the Customize button shows up. If you don't see the Customize button, tap and hold the Lock Screen again, and then enter your passcode.

Personalize a Lock Screen background with filters, widgets, and styles

- In the Settings application, choose Wallpaper.
- Tap Customize under the preview of your Lock Screen.
- Select a wallpaper by tapping Customize Current Wallpaper or Adding a New Wallpaper.
- Make modifications to the wallpaper before tapping Done.
- Tap the time to select a font and text color.
- Tap the boxes above or below the time to add or delete widgets, such as Calendar, Clock, Weather, Fitness, and Reminders.
- Swipe left or right to apply picture styles such as Black & White, Duotone, and Color Wash.
- To trim and relocate your image, squeeze and drag it.

- To access wallpaper selection choices, hit More. Perspective Zoom adjusts the wallpaper as the screen is tilted. Depth Effect permits stacking with your photo's topic.

MODIFY THE RINGTONE ON IPHONE

- Locate and launch the Settings app
- Select the Sounds and Touch option
- Select Ringtone
- Select a different ringtone to hear it.
- Use it

USE DARK MODE ON THE IPHONE.

- Enable Dark Mode for an optimal viewing experience in low-light settings.
- Enable Dark Mode in Settings or the Control Panel
- Select Settings followed by Display & Brightness.

Choose Dark to enable Dark Mode.

To enable and disable Dark Mode in Control Center:

- Tap Settings followed by Control Center.
- To add Dark Mode to Control Center, tap the Add button beside it.

CONFIGURE DARK MODE TO ACTIVATE AUTOMATICALLY

- Select Settings followed by Display & Brightness.
- Select Automatic.
- To establish a timetable for Dark Mode, tap Options.

SET AN IPHONE PASSCODE

Set a passcode that must be input to unlock iPhone when it is turned on or awakened for more security. Setting a passcode enables data protection, which encrypts iPhone data using 256-bit AES encryption. (Some applications may choose not to use data protection.)

CONFIGURE OR MODIFY THE PASSCODE

Navigate to Settings and do one of the following:

- On an iPhone equipped with Face ID, choose Face ID & Passcode.
- Tap Enable Password or Change Password.

Tap Passcode Choices to explore password creation options. Custom Alphanumeric Code and Custom Numeric Code are the most secure alternatives.

After setting a passcode, you may unlock your iPhone using Face ID In the following circumstances, you must always input your password to unlock your iPhone for further security:

You activate or restart the iPhone.

- Your iPhone has not been unlocked for more than 48 hours.

You have not unlocked your iPhone using the password in the previous 6.5 days, and you have not used Face ID

- Your iPhone gets an order to lock remotely.

There have been five failed Face ID attempts to unlock your iPhone.

- An effort is made to use Emergency SOS
- An attempt is made to view your Medical ID

CHANGE WHEN IPHONE LOCKS AUTOMATICALLY

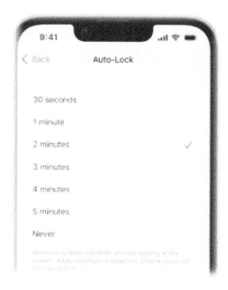

Go to Settings, then Display & Brightness, then Auto-Lock, and pick a time.

ERASE DATA AFTER 10 UNSUCCESSFUL PASSCODES

Configure iPhone to delete all data, media, and personal settings after 10 unsuccessful passcodes try.

Navigate to Settings and do one of the following:

On an iPhone equipped with Face ID, choose Face ID & Passcode.

Scroll to the bottom of the page and choose Erase Data.

DISABLE THE PASSCODE

Navigate to Settings and do one of the following:

On an iPhone equipped with Face ID, choose Face ID & Passcode.

- Tap Disable Passcode.

CHANGE THE PASSCODE

If you input the incorrect passcode six times in succession, you will be locked out of your smartphone and see an "iPhone is disabled" notice. If you forget your passcode, you may delete your iPhone using a computer or recovery mode, and then establish a new password.

Note: If you backed up your data and settings to iCloud or your computer before forgetting your passcode, you may restore your data and settings from the backup.

CONFIGURE FACE ID ON AN IPHONE

Use Face ID (on compatible models) to quickly and securely unlock your iPhone, approve purchases and payments, and log in to a variety of third-party applications with just a glance.

You must also set up a passcode on your iPhone to use Face ID.

CONFIGURE FACE ID OR ADD A SUBSTITUTE APPEARANCE

If you didn't set up Face ID when you first set up your iPhone, go to Settings > Face ID & Passcode > Set up Face ID and follow the on-screen instructions.

- To configure an alternate look for Face ID to recognize, go to Settings > Face ID & Passcode > Set Up an Alternative Appearance and then follow the on-screen instructions.
- During Face ID setup, you may choose Accessibility Options if you have physical constraints. Setting up face recognition in this manner does not need the complete range of head movements. Face ID remains safe, but it demands more consistency in how you look at your iPhone.

Face ID also has an accessibility feature for people who have low vision or none at all. To stop Face ID from making you stare at your iPhone with your eyes open, go to Settings > Accessibility and turn off Require Attention for Face ID. If VoiceOver is turned on after the first time you set up your iPhone, this function is turned off automatically.

FACE ID MAY BE USED WHILE WEARING A FACE MASK.

On iPhone 14 models, you can use Face ID to unlock your phone while wearing a face mask (or other covering that blocks your mouth and nose).

- When you use Face ID with a Mask, it looks at the unique features around your eyes. It works with all Face ID settings in Settings > Face ID & Passcode.
- Face ID works best when it only recognizes the whole face.

Navigate to Settings > Face ID & Passcode, then do one of the following actions:

Allow Face ID to function with a face mask: Follow the instructions on the screen to turn on Face ID with a Mask.

Important: If you usually wear glasses, wearing clear glasses (not shades) while using Face ID with a Mask may help it work better.

Transparent glasses (not sunglasses) should be added to your appearance: Tap "Add Glasses," then do what it says on the screen.

Face ID should not function when wearing a face mask: If you are wearing a mask, turn off Face ID.

On the other hand, any Face ID-enabled iPhone model can be unlocked with an Apple Watch while wearing a face mask.

TEMPORARILY TURN OFF FACE ID

You can stop Face ID from unlocking your iPhone temporarily.

- Hold the side button and either volume button for two seconds.
- When the sliders appear, quickly lock the iPhone by pressing the button on the side.
- After about a minute of not being used, the iPhone locks itself.

Face ID will work again the next time you use your passcode to open your iPhone.

DISABLE FACE ID

Navigate to the Settings > Face ID & Passcode menu.

Perform one of the subsequent:

Turn off Face ID just for certain items: Deactivate one or more options.

Disable Face ID for masks: With a mask on, turn off Face ID.

To turn off Face ID, tap "Reset Face ID."

Where's My iPhone? You can stop Face ID from being used to unlock your phone if it gets lost or stolen with Lost Mode.

MANAGE ACCESS TO THE IPHONE LOCK SCREEN'S CONTENT

From the Lock Screen, you may instantly access a few frequently used functions (such as widgets, media playback controls, and Control Center). When iPhone is locked, you may manage access to these things. (When the iPhone is locked, USB connections are not permitted for security reasons.)

By turning off access to a feature from the Lock Screen, you stop anyone who has access to your iPhone from reading any personal information it might have (such as an upcoming event in the Calendar widget). But it's harder to get to your information.

Choose what you want below. Go to Settings > Face ID & Passcode to allow access when the phone is locked (on an iPhone with Face ID)

You may enable or disable access to the following iPhone functionalities when the device is locked:

- Widgets
- Notification Facility
- Control Center
- Siri
- Responding to messaging
- Home Automation
- Wallet
- Calling back missed calls
- USB connectivity to a Mac, Windows PC, or accessories

Important: If you modify the default option to enable USB connections when the iPhone is locked, you eliminate a crucial iPhone security safeguard.

Additionally, you may provide medical information and emergency contacts in a Medical ID that first responders and others can read on your locked iPhone.

CHAPTER FIVE

MAKE AN IPHONE CALL.

To initiate a call in the Phone app, dial the number on the keyboard, touch a recent or favorite call, or choose a contact.

- Dial a number

Say "call" or "dial" followed by a number to Siri. Speak each numeral individually, such as "four one five, five five five..." For the 800 area code in the United States, you may say "800." Discover how to use Siri.

Alternatively, do the following:

- Tap Keyboard.

9:41

Primary ——————— Make the call
on another lin

1	2	3
4	5	6
7	8	9
*	0	#

Perform any of the subsequent:

Use a different line: Touch the line at the top of Dual SIM devices and then choose a line.

Enter the number through the numeric keypad: If you make an error, touch the Delete key.

Dial the previous number: Press the Call button to see the most recent number you phoned, then tap the Call button again to dial that number.

Copy a number and then paste it: Tap the phone number field above the keyboard, followed by Paste.

84

Insert a two-second pause: Touch and hold the star (*) key until you see a comma.

Enter a hard pause (to halt dialing until the Dial button is pressed): Touch and hold the pound (#) key until you see a semicolon.

For international calls, type "+" Hold the "o" key until the "+" symbol appears.

- Touch the Call button to initiate a call.
- Tap the Terminate Call button to end a call.

Call your favorites

- Tap Favorites, and then choose the person you want to call.

On phones with two SIM cards, the iPhone chooses which line to use for a call in the following order:

- This person chose this phone number (if set)
- The number of the last call this contact made or received.
- The usual voice track

Choose from the following to manage your Favorites list:

Add a favorite: Tap the Add button before selecting a contact.

Rearrange or remove favorites: Tap Edit.

Call back or redial a recent call.

Siri: Say "Call that number again" or "Call me back" Find out how to use Siri.

Moreover, you may accomplish the following:

Tap Recents, then choose a contact to call.

Change your outgoing call configuration

- Navigate to Settings > Phone.

Perform any of the subsequent:

Turn on Display My Caller Identification: Your phone number is shown by (GSM) My Number. Even if caller ID is turned off, FaceTime calls to show your phone number.

Enable Dial Assist while making international calls: (GSM) When Dial Assist is on, iPhone inserts the right international or local prefix when calling contacts and favorites.

Contact your carrier for details on making international calls, including applicable rates and additional fees.

ANSWER OR REFUSE INCOMING IPHONE CALLS

You may answer an incoming call, hush it, or refuse it. If you refuse a call, it goes to voicemail. You may react with a text message or remind yourself to call back.

Accept a call

Perform one of the subsequent:

- Select the Accept Call button.

If the iPhone is locked, you must drag the slider.

Siri can announce incoming calls, which you may either accept or reject with your voice.

Silence a call

- Press either the volume button or the side button.

A hushed call may still be answered until it gets to voicemail.

Refuse a call and route it to voicemail.

- **Perform one of the subsequent**:
- Double-tap the side button rapidly.
- Tap the button labeled Reject Call.
- Swipe the call banner upwards.

Additionally, you may swipe down on the call banner for additional choices.

Perform any of the subsequent:

- Tap "Remind Me," and then choose when you want to be reminded to call back.
- Tap Message then chooses a canned answer or tap Custom.
- To make your default responses, go to Settings > Phone > Respond with Text, then press any default message and type your text in its place.

In some countries or places, calls that are turned down are ended right away instead of being sent to voicemail.

CHOOSE IPHONE RINGTONES AND VIBRATIONS

You may change the default ringtone and apply unique ringtones to individual contacts. Additionally, you may use vibrations and disable the ringer.

MODIFY ALERT TONES AND VIBRATIONS

The iPhone has ringtones for incoming calls. Additionally, you may buy additional ringtones from the iTunes Store.

Assign a different ringtone to a contact

- Launch the Contacts program.
- Choose a contact, then choose Edit, Ringtone, then a ringtone.

ADJUST THE RINGER'S STATUS.

Flip the Ring/Quiet switch to enable or disable silent mode. When the quiet mode is enabled, clock alarms continue to play.

To temporarily muffle incoming calls, Activate or schedule a Focus on iPhone session.

AVOID UNSOLICITED IPHONE CALLS

You may prevent receiving unwanted calls by banning certain numbers and routing unknown and spam callers straight to voicemail.

Prevent phone calls, FaceTime calls, and messages from certain individuals.

In the Phone app, you may do any of the following actions:

Choose from Favorites, Recents, and Voicemail. Hit the More Info icon beside the number or contact you want to block, then scroll down and tap Block this Caller.

- Touch Contacts, then hit the contact whose calls you want to block, scroll down, and then tap Block this Caller.

CONTROL BANNED CONTACTS

- Go to Phone Settings > Blocked Contacts.
- Tap Edit.

Forward unknown and unsolicited calls to voicemail

Navigate to Settings > Phone, then choose one of the options below.

You get alerts for calls from persons in your contacts, recent outgoing calls, and Siri Suggestions while Unknown Callers are muted.

Call Blocking & Identification: To mute calls recognized by your carrier as suspected spam or fraud, activate Silence Junk Callers (available with certain carriers).

CHAPTER SIX

FACETIME

With an internet connection and an Apple ID, it is possible to make and receive FaceTime calls.

FaceTime must be configured before calls may be made or received.

FaceTime calls may also be made via a cellular data connection, which may involve extra fees. To disable this function, go to Settings > Cellular and then disable FaceTime.

CONDUCT A FACETIME CALL.

Turn off your mic.

Turn off your camera.

Drag your image to any corner.

Add stickers and other fun effects.

Switch to the rear camera.

Say something like "Make a FaceTime call" to Siri. Discover how to use Siri.

Tap New FaceTime towards the top of the FaceTime screen.

Input the desired person or number in the input area at the top, then touch FaceTime or Call to initiate a video or audio call, respectively (not available in all countries or regions).

Alternately, you may hit the Add Contact button to open Contacts and add individuals from there, or you can select a recommended contact from your call history to place a call immediately.

Tip: To view more during a FaceTime video conversation, rotate your iPhone to use the landscape position.

RECEIVE A FACETIME CALL

When a FaceTime call arrives, do one of the following actions:

Accept the call: Slide the slider or choose Accept.

- Refuse the call by tapping Decline.

Tap Remind Me to set a callback reminder.

Tap Message to send a text message to the caller.

Instead of Accept, you see End & Accept if you're on another call and a FaceTime call arrives, which cancels the current connection and connects you to the incoming call.

Siri can announce incoming calls, which you may either accept or reject with your voice.

FaceTime calls may be initiated via a Messages discussion.

You may initiate a FaceTime call with the person you're conversing with using Messages.

Tap the FaceTime button in the upper-right corner of the chat window.

Perform any of the subsequent:

- Tap FaceTime Audio.
- Tap FaceTime Video.

Leave a message

If no one answers your FaceTime call, you may either:

- Select Leave Message.
- Tap Cancel.

Select Call Back.

- Call again

From your call history, tap the name or number of the person (or group) you want to call again.

ELIMINATE A CALL FROM YOUR CALL LOG.

Swipe left over the call in FaceTime's call history, then hit Delete.

TAKE A FACETIME LIVE PHOTO ON AN IPHONE

During a FaceTime video chat, you may snap a FaceTime Live Photo to save a moment of the discussion (not available in all countries or regions). The camera records what occurs immediately before and after the picture is taken, as well as the audio, so that you may see and hear everything exactly as it occurred.

FaceTime Live Photos must be enabled in Settings > FaceTime before you may capture a FaceTime Live Photo.

On a call with a single other participants, tap the Capture Image button.

Press the tile of the person you want to picture, then tap the Full Screen and Take Picture buttons during a Group FaceTime session.

You and your subject get a notice that the picture has been shot, and the Live Photo is stored in your Photos app.

MAKE AN IPHONE GROUP FACETIME CALL

In the FaceTime app, up to 32 people can join a Group FaceTime chat (not available in all countries or regions).

Start a FaceTime Group call

- Tap New FaceTime towards the top of the FaceTime screen.
- Input the names or phone numbers of the individuals you like to call in the box at the top.

Additionally, you may touch the Add Contact icon to access Contacts and add individuals from there. Or choose recommended contacts from the call log.

Tap the FaceTime icon to initiate a FaceTime video call, or the Call icon to initiate a FaceTime audio call.

Each participant is represented as a tile on the display. When a participant talks (verbally or via sign language) or you touch a tile, it becomes more prominent. The excess tiles display in a row at the bottom of the screen. To locate an absent participant, swipe through the row. (If no picture is available, the participant's initials will show on the tile.)

To avoid the tile of the person speaking or signing during a Group FaceTime session from getting bigger, go to Settings > FaceTime and disable Speaking below Automatic Prominence.

Note: Sign language identification needs a presenter-supported model. Moreover, both the presenter and participants must have iOS 14, iPadOS 14, or macOS 11 or a later version.

GROUP FACETIME CALLS MAY BE INITIATED VIA A GROUP MESSAGES DISCUSSION.

In a group Messages discussion, you may initiate a Group FaceTime call with everyone in the conversation.

Tap the FaceTime button in the upper-right corner of the chat window.

Perform any of the subsequent:

- Tap FaceTime Audio.
- Tap FaceTime Video.

Add a participant to a call

- Any person on a FaceTime call can add another person at any time.
- During a FaceTime conversation, press the screen to show the FaceTime controls (if they aren't already showing), then press the More Info button and Add People.
- Enter the name, Apple ID, or phone number of the person you want to add in the box at the top.
- To add a contact from Contacts, you can also press the Add Contact icon.
- Choose "Add People."

JOIN A FACETIME GROUP CALL.

When someone asks you to join a Group FaceTime call, you are notified of the incoming call and can accept or decline the invitation. See Receive a FaceTime call.

Hang up on a Group FaceTime call

- Tap Leave at any time to end a group call.

- If there are still at least two people on the call, it will go on.

iPhone users can end a FaceTime call or switch to Messages.

At any point, you may end a FaceTime call or transfer the discussion to Messages.

LEAVE A FACETIME CALL

Hit the display to see the FaceTime controls (if they're not already visible), then tap the Leave Call button.

SWITCH TO A CHAT IN MESSAGES

To access a Messages thread that includes everyone in the conversation, press the screen to reveal the FaceTime controls (if they are not already visible), hit the Info button at the top of the controls, and then tap Message or the Open Messages button.

BLOCK UNSOLICITED FACETIME CALLS ON IPHONE

In the FaceTime application, you may ban unsolicited FaceTime calls.

- Tap the Info button next to the name, phone number, or email address of the person you want to block in your FaceTime call history.

- Scroll down and choose Block this Caller followed by Block Contact.
- Choose the contact that you want to block.

To unblock a contact, press the Info button next to their name, phone number, or email address in your call record, scroll down, and then tap Unblock this Caller.

CHAPTER SEVEN

SEND AND RECEIVE IPHONE TEXTS

Use the Communications application to send and receive text, image, video, and audio messages.

Send a message from the nearest device, then use Handoff to continue the discussion on another device.

Send a message

You may initiate a discussion with one or more persons through text message.

To compose a new message, hit the Compose button at the top of the screen, or tap an existing message.

Enter each recipient's phone number, contact name, or Apple ID. Alternatively, touch the Add button and choose contacts.

If Dual SIM is enabled on a suitable model and you want to send an SMS/MMS message from a separate line, press the displayed line and then choose the other line.

Hit the text area, then tap the Send button to send your message.

A blue send button indicates that the message will be delivered through iMessage; a green send button denotes that the message will be sent via SMS/MMS or your cellular connection.

An alert If a message cannot be transmitted, a warning badge displays. Tap the notification to resend the message.

Instead of typing out your message by hand, you can press the Dictation button and speak it.

To see chat information, tap the name or phone number at the top of the screen. Touching the contact lets you do things like change the contact card, share your location, see attachments, and leave a group chat.

To get back to the list of messages from a chat, press the Back button or swipe left.

Continue a discussion

When someone sends you their first message, a discussion begins. If you have already communicated with this person in Messages, their message is appended to the conclusion of the previous chat.

- Tap the discussion you want to take part in on the Messages list.
- Press the search bar above the Messages lists to look for people and conversational content. (Swiping down may be needed to see the search area.) Also, the search area shows suggested contacts, websites, photos, and other things.
- Tap the text box and type what you want to say. To replace highlighted text with emoji, choose Next Keyboard, Emoji, or Next Keyboard and then tap each highlighted word.

- Click the Send button to send your message.
- Go to Settings > Messages and turn on Send Read Receipts to let people know you've read their messages.
- When you drag a message bubble to the left, you can see when it was sent or received.

Respond to a particular message inside a chat.

In group or individual chats, you may react to a single message inline to increase clarity and keep the topic structured.

- Touch and hold a message in a chat, then hit the Reply button.
- Enter your answer and then click the Send button.

Using the term "Tapback," you can quickly reply to messages (for example, a thumbs-up or a heart). Tap the message bubble you want to respond to twice, and then tap Tapback.

SEND AN AUDIO MESSAGE RECORDING

Instead of typing a text message, you may rapidly record an audio message that can be played from inside the discussion in Messages.

Recording audio is an iMessage application. Press the Apps button in a Messages discussion to display the app icons below the text field, tap the Audio Recording button, and then perform one of the following:

- To document and evaluate before sending: To initiate recording, tap the Record button. Hit the Play button to listen to the recording, then tap the Send button to send or the Cancel button to cancel.
- To record a message and quickly transmit it, press and hold the Record button.
- Two minutes after you send an audio message, it will vanish from your chat unless you hit Keep. Still, recipients may play your recording. To preserve audio messages forever, go to Settings > Messages > Expire (below Audio Messages) and hit Never.
- FaceTime may be used to make audio or video calls instead of sending text messages. Tap the FaceTime button inside a chat in Messages.

LISTEN TO OR RESPOND TO AN AUDIO RECORDING

Raise the iPhone to your ear to hear incoming voicemails.

- Raise it once more to respond.
- To enable or disable this function, go to Settings > Messages and toggle Raise to Listen.

Transmit SMS messages to more devices

When you send a message to a user of a device other than an iPhone, the message is transmitted as an SMS. You may configure your iPhone so that SMS messages sent or received show on your other devices.

- Navigate: Settings > Messages
- Tap Text Message Forwarding, then activate the desired devices.

If you are not using two-factor authentication, a six-digit activation number will display on your other device; input this code on your iPhone and then hit Allow.

USE IMESSAGE APPLICATIONS IN IPHONE MESSAGES

Browse iMessage app

Through iMessage applications, you may embellish a chat with stickers, play a game, and exchange tunes without leaving the Messages app. You may enhance your messaging capabilities by installing additional iMessage applications from the App Store.

EXPLORE AND DOWNLOAD THE IMESSAGE APPLICATION

- Tap the Apps button during a Messages discussion to see the app icons below the text field.
- Tap the Store button to launch the iMessage App Store.
- Press an app to explore further information and user reviews, then hit the price to buy it or tap Get to download it for free.
- All purchases are performed using the Apple ID-associated payment mechanism.

Employ an iMessage app.

- Tap the Apps button during a Messages discussion to see the app icons below the text field.
- Tap an iMessage application, then choose an item to include in a message bubble.
- Add a remark (optional), then touch the Send or Remove button to send or cancel your message.

MANAGE IMESSAGE APPLICATIONS

Swipe right on the app icons below the text field in a Messages chat, then press the More button.

- Tap Edit, then do any of the following actions using your iMessage applications:
- Reorder applications by dragging the Reorder button.

Include an application in Favorites: Select the Add icon.

Delete an application from Favorites: Select the Delete key.

To hide an application, turn it off.

Delete an app: Swipe the app to the left, and then choose Remove from Favorites. Swipe the app again to the left, then press Delete.

USE MEMOJI IN IPHONE MESSAGES

Use the Messages app to express yourself with Memoji and customized sticker packs of Memoji that correspond to your personality and mood. On devices with a TrueDepth camera, you can send animated Memoji messages that reflect your facial emotions and capture your voice.

CREATE A CUSTOM MEMOJI

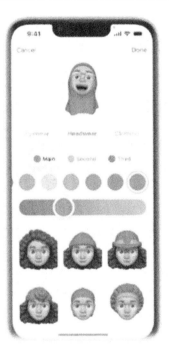

You may create your own customized Memoji by selecting skin tone, headgear, and other attributes. You may make several Memoji for various emotions.

- Hit the Memoji Stickers button in a discussion, then tap the New Memoji button.
- Tap each feature and set the parameters you want. As you give your Memoji more traits, your character starts to take shape.
- Tap Done to add the Memoji to your collection.

- To change, copy, or get rid of a Memoji, press the Memoji Stickers button, press the Memoji, and then press the More Options button.

SEND MEMOJI AND MEMOJI STICKERS
Messages produce sticker packs automatically based on your Memoji and Memoji characters. You may communicate a variety of emotions in novel ways with stickers.

- Tap the Memoji Stickers icon inside a discussion.
- To display the sticker pack's stickers, choose a Memoji from the top row.

Send a sticker by any of the following methods:

- To add a sticker to the message bubble, tap the sticker. If desired, add a remark, then hit the Submit button to send.
- Touch and hold a sticker before dragging it into a discussion message. The sticker is automatically delivered when it is added to a message.

SEND A DIGITAL TOUCH EFFECT IN IPHONE MESSAGES

Digital Touch allows you to send animated doodles, taps, kisses, heartbeats, and more inside an iMessage discussion in the Messages app. A Digital Touch effect may also be applied to a picture or video.

Send a drawing.

- In the app drawer, tap the Digital Touch icon.
- Tap the color dot to choose a color, then use one finger to draw.
- You may alter the color before beginning to sketch again.
- To send your message, hit the Send button, and to erase it, tap the Delete button.

Describe your emotions

In the app drawer, tap the Digital Touch icon.

Send one of the following animations through canvas gestures. Your emotions are sent immediately after you complete the gesture:

Tap: Tap with one finger to generate a colorful explosion. You can adjust the color and then tap again.

- Touch and hold the fireball with one finger.
- Tap with two fingers to kiss.
- Touch and hold the heartbeat with two fingers.
- Touch and hold with two fingers until a heartbeat appears, then pull down to shatter the heart.

Note: If you have an Apple Watch or another sensor that tracks your heartbeat, Messages may use this information when you send a Digital Touch heartbeat.

APPLY THE DIGITAL TOUCH EFFECT TO AN IMAGE OR VIDEO.

- In the app drawer, tap the Digital Touch icon.
- Tap the button labeled Camera.
- Tap the Snap Picture or Record Video button to take a picture or record a video, respectively.

Include a Digital Touch effect, such as a kiss or a doodle.

To send your message, hit the Send button; to remove it, tap the Close button.

CHAPTER EIGHT

BROWSE THE WEB USING SAFARI ON IPHONE

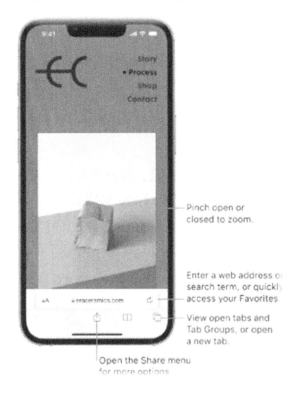

Pinch open or closed to zoom.

Enter a web address or search term, or quickly access your Favorites

View open tabs and Tab Groups, or open a new tab.

Open the Share menu for more options

In the Safari app, you may surf the web, see websites, preview website links, translate webpages, and reinstall the Safari app if it is deleted from your Home Screen. Sign in to iCloud on several devices with the same Apple ID to synchronize your open tabs, bookmarks, history, and Reading List across all of your devices.

BROWSE THE INTERNET USING SAFARI

A few touches are sufficient to explore a website with ease.

Return to the summit: Double-tap the screen's upper border to rapidly return to the top of a lengthy page.

View more content: Orient your iPhone in landscape mode.

Reloading the page: From the top of the page, pull it down.

Tap the Share button at the bottom of the page to share links.

Preview website links

Touch and hold a link to see the URL and these options.

Safari allows you to get a preview of a link without opening the website by touching and holding a link. To open the link, choose Open or touch the link's preview.

To dismiss the preview and return to the current page, touch outside the preview.

Translate a website or picture.

When viewing a foreign-language website or picture, Safari may translate the text for you (not available in all languages or regions).

The Page Settings button is followed by the Translate button (if the translation is available).

RESTORE SAFARI TO YOUR HOME SCREEN

If Safari is missing from your Home Screen, you may locate it in the App Library and reinstall it.

- Swipe left on the Home Screen to open the App Library.
- Input "Safari" into the search box.
- Tap Add to Home Screen after pressing and holding the Safari icon.

CUSTOMIZE YOUR IPHONE'S SAFARI SETTINGS

You may modify your Safari layout, start page, and font size on websites, as well as display and privacy settings using the Safari app. Sign in to iCloud on several devices with the same Apple ID to synchronize your open tabs, bookmarks, history, and Reading List across all of your devices.

CUSTOMIZE YOUR START PAGE

When you open a new tab, you are sent to your homepage. You may change the background pictures and choices on your homepage.

- Tap the Tabs icon, followed by the New Tab icon.
- Tap Edit then scrolls to the bottom of the page.
- Select choices for your homepage.

Use Home Page on All Devices: Maintain your settings and preferences across all Apple devices where your Apple ID is logged in.

Tab Group Favorites: View and access frequently-used tab groups quickly.

Recently Closed Tabs: Reopen previously closed tabs.

Favorites: Display links to your bookmarked favorite websites. See Bookmark a favorite website.

Siri Suggestions: Allow webpages shared in Calendar and other applications to surface when you search.

Presented to You: View links exchanged in Messages, Mail, and elsewhere. See Locate shared links in Safari on your iPhone.

Go directly to the websites you visit most often.

Privacy Report: Track the number of trackers and websites that Safari has prevented from monitoring you. See View the Report on Privacy.

Reading List: Display the websites in your Reading List. See Add this page to your Reading List.

iCloud Tabs: Display open tabs from other Apple devices when the same Apple ID is logged in and Safari is enabled in iCloud settings or preferences. **See Organize your iPhone Safari tabs using Tab Groups.**

Background Picture: Select the image that will display in the background whenever a new start page is opened in this Tab Group.

Your custom start page settings are updated across all Apple devices when Use Start Page on All Devices is enabled and you are logged in with the same Apple ID using two-factor authentication.

MODIFY TEXT SIZE

- Use the Page Settings button to adjust the font size.
- The Page Settings button is located to the left of the search box.
- Tap the big A or the tiny A to raise or reduce the text size, respectively.

MODIFY DISPLAY AND PRIVACY SETTINGS

You may switch to Reader, conceal the search area, and configure privacy settings for a website, among other things.

Tap the Page Settings button, then do any of the below actions:

View the website without advertisements or menus: Tap Display Reader (if available).

Cover the search box: Tap Hide Toolbar (tap the top of the screen to get it back).

Examine the website's appearance on a desktop computer: Select Request Desktop Site (if available).

Configure the display and privacy settings for each visit to this website: Tap Website Settings.

HOW TO PERSONALIZE IPHONE SAFARI

You may install extensions in the Safari app to alter how your browser functions. Extensions may, for instance, help you locate discounts while shopping, restrict material on websites, and provide access to the functionality of other programs.

VIEW AND INSTALL SAFARI EXTENSIONS

- Navigate to Settings > Safari > Extensions.
- Tap More Extensions to peruse the App Store's extensions.

Press the pricing, or if the application is free, tap Get, and then follow the on-screen instructions.

MANAGE YOUR EXTENSIONS

Hit Page Settings to the left of the search area, and then tap Manage Extensions. Select or deselect each extension to enable or disable it.

HOW TO USE SAFARI EXTENSIONS

The content of the websites you visit is accessed by extensions. You may modify the level of access granted to each extension:

Tap the Page Settings option to the left of the search bar, then tap the extension for which you want to provide rights.

Choose the level of access for each extension.

Check the extensions you have installed and familiarize yourself with their functionality.

DELETE A FILE EXTENSION

- Swipe down on the Home Screen, and then search for the extension you want to uninstall.
- Touch and hold the icon for the extension, hit the Delete app, and then follow the on-screen instructions.

HIDE ADS AND DISTRACTIONS IN SAFARI ON IPHONE

Tap to view the

Use Reader inside Safari to conceal advertisements, navigation menus, and other distracting elements.

Show Viewer

- Reader prepares a website so that just the relevant text and pictures are shown.
- Tap the Page Settings button, followed by the Show Reader button.

- To return to the whole page, touch Page Settings followed by hiding Reader.

If Show Reader is disabled, Reader is not accessible for the current page.

USE READER AUTOMATICALLY FOR A WEBPAGE.

Hit the Page Settings icon, then tap Website Settings on a compatible website.

- SET USE READER AUTOMATICALLY TO ON.

Note: To use Reader automatically on all pages that accept it, go to Settings > Safari > Reader.

BLOCK POP-UPS

Go to Settings > Safari, then enable Pop-up Blocking.

CHAPTER NINE

CAMERA FEATURES ON IPHONE

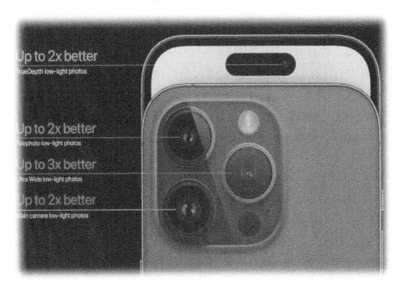

Discover the iPhone's Photographic Styles, QuickTake, Action mode, Ultra Wide camera, and other camera functions.

Photographic Styles will lock in your look.

With Photographic Styles, the Camera app on iPhone 14 pro max and iPhone 14 pro allow you to customize the appearance of your photographs. Choose a default — Rich Contrast, Vibrant, Warm, or Cool — then, if desired, change the Tone and Warmth settings for more customization. Set your chosen style once, and it will be used each time you snap a shot in Photo mode.

Establish a Photographic Mode

When you initially launch the Camera app, press Setup to select your Photographic Style. Swipe through the various styles and hit Use [Style Name] on the desired preset.

Make careful you pick your style before you begin shooting images; you cannot add your Photographic Style to an image that has already been captured.

Alter your photographic mode.

Want to change the style of photography you chose? Just open the Camera app, press the arrow button, and then choose Photographic Styles. Standard is the basic, balanced style that looks like real life and can't be changed. However, you can swipe left to see other preset styles that can be changed. Tap Customize to change the style you've chosen's Tone and Warmth.

Use macro photography and video to get close-ups.

Macro photography is possible with the new Ultra-Wide camera and improved lens and auto-focus technology on the iPhone 14 Pro and 14 Pro Max. This lets you take amazing close-ups with sharp focus up to 2 cm away. Also, the iPhone 14Pro and iPhone 14 Pro Max can record macro movies, including slow-motion and time-lapse.

In Photo and Video modes, shooting macro is done automatically. Move your iPhone close to the subject, and if the Ultra Wide camera isn't already selected, the camera will switch to it while keeping your composition. To record macro slow-motion or time-lapse videos, choose the Ultra Wide camera (0.5x) and move in close to the subject.

When you move your iPhone closer to or farther from a subject, you'll notice that the Camera app changes to the Ultra Wide camera. By going to Settings > Camera > Macro Control, you can change how the automatic macro switching works. When Macro Control is turned on, when the subject is close enough, the Camera app on your iPhone shows a macro button. Tap the macro button once to turn off auto-switching between macros, then tap it again to turn it back on.

If you turn on Macro Control, the camera will switch to macro mode automatically the next time you use it at a macro distance. Go to Settings > Camera > Preserve Settings and turn on Macro Control to keep your Macro Control setting between camera sessions.

Capture a video with QuickTake

QuickTake allows users to capture movies without leaving the picture mode.

Hold the shutter button to record a video.

When you open the Camera app, the picturesque setting that was used last time is shown. To take a picture, tap the Shutter button. Then, tap the arrow to change things like flash, Live Photos, and the timer.

Just press and hold the Shutter button to make a QuickTake video. When you let go of the button, the recording session is over.

To lock the recording, slide to the right

Move the Shutter button to the right and then let go of it to keep recording without holding the button down. When the video recording is turned off, a button that says "Shutter" will appear on the right. During video recording, tap the Shutter button to take a still picture. When you're ready to stop recording, tap the record button.

Slide to the left to activate burst mode.

Slide the Shutter button to the left and hold it to take a series of pictures, then let go of the button to stop.

With iOS 14 and later, you can use the Volume up button to take multiple photos at once. Use the Use Volume Up for Burst setting, which can be found in Settings > Camera.

Action mode provides a more stable video capture

With the iPhone 14pro max and iPhone 14 Pro's Action mode, you can record smooth video while you're moving, even if you're holding the phone in your hand.

Launch the Camera app and tap the Video mode button.

- To start Action mode, touch the button.
- Tap the "Shutter" button to start making a video.

In the Action mode, the camera will show "More light needed" if there is not enough light. Change the settings on your camera so that Action mode works when there isn't much light.

Tap Camera in the Settings application.

- Tap Record Video.
- Turn on Action Mode and Put out the Light.

In action mode, you can record at 60 frames per second in 1080p or 2.8k. The iPhone 14 Pro, works with both Dolby Vision HDR and Apple ProRes video formats.

Adjust your focus and exposure

Before taking a picture, the camera automatically adjusts the focus and exposure. Face recognition also adjusts the exposure so that it is balanced across many faces. Exposure Compensation Control can be used to control and lock the exposure so that it will be the same for all future photos.

To change the exposure level, just press the arrow and tap. You can't change the exposure until you open the Camera app again.

Take a reflective selfie

With iOS 14 or later, you can take mirrored selfies that record the image exactly as it looks in the camera frame. Go to Settings > Camera and turn on the option to use the Mirror Front Camera.

Capture photographs even quicker

You can change how photos are processed by using the Prioritize Faster Shooting set. This lets you take more photos when you quickly press the Shutter button. Go to Settings > Camera and turn off Prioritize Faster Shooting to turn this feature off.

Prioritize Faster Shooting is available on iOS 16 and later devices, the iPhone 14 Pro, and the iPhone 14 Pro Max.

Improve selfies and Ultra Wide images

Lens Correction makes the image look more natural when you take a selfie with the front-facing camera or a picture with the Ultra Wide (0.5x) lens. Go to Settings > Camera and turn off Lens Correction to turn this off.

Do more with your iPhone's camera

Need to take photographs in low-light settings? Learn how to use Night Mode on iPhone models that support it.

Use Live Photos to capture moving and audible events.

Apple ProRAW allows users more creative flexibility when editing photographs.

IPHONE CAMERA BASICS

Learn how to use the Camera app on your iPhone. To frame your image, choose from modes such as Photo, Video, Cinematic, Pano, and Portrait, and zoom in or out.

Open Camera

To launch the Camera, do one of the following:

- Tap Camera on the Home screen of the iPhone.
- On the iPhone Lock Screen, swipe left.
- Touch and hold the Camera button on the Lock Screen of the iPhone.
- Tap the Camera button after opening Control Center.

Siri: Say something like: "Open Camera." Discover how to use Siri.

Note: A green dot displays in the upper-right corner of the screen while the Camera is active for your safety.

Take a picture

To snap a photo, launch Camera, then hit the Shutter button or push either volume button.

How To Select From Camera Modes

Photo is the default mode shown when you launch the Camera. Use the Photo mode to capture both still and moving images. Swipe the screen to the left or right to choose one of the following camera modes:

Video: Record a video;

- Create a time-lapse film showing motion over an extended period;

Slo-mo: Record a video in slow motion;

- Take a panoramic photograph of a landscape or other subject;
- Use a depth-of-field effect on your portraits (on devices that support it);

Cinematic: Apply a depth-of-field effect to your films (on models supported);

- Take photographs with a square aspect ratio.

138

Hit the Camera Controls button, then tap 4:3 to toggle between square, 4:3, and 16:9 aspect ratios on iPhone 14 pro and later.

See Save camera settings on iPhone to make a mode other than Photo the default when you open Camera.

THE ABILITY TO ZOOM IN OR OUT.
On all models, open the Camera app and pinch the screen to zoom in or out.

Choose between 0.5x, 1x, 2x, 2.5x, and 3x on iPhone models with Dual and Triple camera systems to easily zoom in or out (depending on your model). For a more precise zoom, touch and hold the zoom controls, then move the slider to the left or right.

USE IPHONE CAMERA FEATURES TO COMPOSE YOUR IMAGE.
You may use Camera tools to alter and enhance your photograph before shooting it.

ADJUST THE FOCUS AND EXPOSURE OF THE CAMERA

Before taking a picture, the iPhone camera automatically adjusts the focus and exposure, and face recognition makes sure that the exposure is the same for all of the faces in the picture. To change the focus and exposure of the camera by hand, do the following:

Open Camera.

- Tap the screen to see where the autofocus is set and what the exposure setting is.
- Tap the place where you want the focus to go.
- To change the exposure, move the Adjust Exposure button up or down next to the area in focus.
- Touch and hold the focus area until you see AE/AF Lock. Press the screen to unlock the settings.

On iPhone 14 pro and subsequent models, it is possible to precisely adjust and lock the exposure for future photos. Tap the Camera Controls button, then the Exposure button, and then drag the exposure slider. The exposure is locked till the next time Camera is opened. Go to Settings > Camera > Preserve Settings and then turn on Exposure Adjustment. This will keep the exposure control from being reset when the Camera is opened.

SWITCH THE FLASH ON OR OFF.

Your iPhone camera is configured to activate the flash automatically when necessary. To manually regulate the flash before taking a photograph, use the steps below:

- Tap the Flash button on iPhone X4 pro, iPhone 14 pro max, and subsequent models to enable or disable the automatic flash. Press the Camera Controls icon, and then tap the Flash icon below the frame to choose Auto, On, or Off.

TAKE A PICTURE WITH A FILTER

Use a filter to impart a color effect to your photograph.

Open the camera, choose the Photo or Portrait mode, and then perform one of the subsequent:

On iPhone 14 pro, iPhone 14pro max, and subsequent models: Tap the Camera Controls icon followed by the Filters icon.

Swipe the filters to the left or right below the viewer to preview them; press one to apply it.

In Photos, you may remove or alter a photo's filter. See Unedit a photograph or video.

USE TIMER

You may set a timer on your iPhone's camera to allow yourself time to position yourself for the photo.

To set a timer, launch Camera and then choose one of the options below:

Press the Camera Controls button, hit the Timer button, choose 3s or 10s, and then tap the Shutter button to start the timer on iPhone 4 pro, iPhone 14 pro max, and later.

USE A GRID TO ALIGN YOUR PHOTO.
To show a grid on the camera's screen to help you align and arrange your shots, to turn on Grid, go to Settings > Camera.

After taking a picture, you can use the editing tools in the Photos app to better align photos and change the horizontal and vertical perspective.

USE PHOTOGRAPHIC STYLES ON THE IPHONE CAMERA

You may apply a Photographic Style to iPhone 14 models, to alter how the Camera takes images. Choose one of the preset styles—Rich Contrast, Vibrant, Warm, or Cool—and then change the tone and warmth parameters to further personalize it. Every time you snap a shot in Photo mode, your settings are applied. In-camera changes and adjustments to Photographic Styles are possible.

SELECT A PHOTOGRAPHIC TECHNIQUE

The camera is automatically set to Standard, a realistic and balanced approach. To apply a distinct Photographic Style, follow the steps below:

- Tap the Camera Controls button after launching the Camera application.
- To sample the various photographic styles, tap the Photographic Styles icon, then slide to the left.

Rich Contrast: Darker shadows, more vibrant colors, and increased contrast provide a dramatic appearance.

- Wonderfully bright and vibrant hues provide a natural but spectacular appearance.
- Golden undertones offer a warmer appearance.
- Blue undertones offer a colder appearance

To modify a Photographic Style, press the Tone and Warmth buttons underneath the frame and then move the slider to the left or right to alter the value. To reset the settings, tap the Reset button next to Photographic Styles.

- To apply a Photographic Style, tap the Photographic Styles icon.
- To modify a previously established Photographic Style, hit the Photographic Styles On button at the top of the display.

In Settings, you may also alter Photographic Styles: go to Options > Camera > Photographic Styles.

TAKE LIVE PHOTOS WITH YOUR IPHONE CAMERA

Use the Camera on the iPhone to shoot Live Photos. A Live Shot captures the audio from the moments right before and after the photo is taken. You snap a Live Photo exactly as you do a conventional photo.

Open Camera.

- Ensure that the Camera is set to Photo mode and that Live Photo is on.

- When Live Photo is enabled, the Live Photo button displays at the top of the display. A vertical line across the Live Photo button indicates that the function is disabled. Tap the button to enable or disable Live Photo.

- To snap a Live Photo, touch the Shutter button.

Tap the picture thumbnail at the bottom of the screen, then touch and hold the screen to play the Live Photo.

HOW TO USE IPHONE CAMERA IN CINEMATIC MODE FOR RECORDING VIDEO

Cinematic mode creates a depth-of-field effect that maintains your video's subject in focus while blurring the foreground and background. iPhone recognizes the topic of the video and maintains it in focus throughout the recording; if a new subject is recognized, iPhone automatically changes the point of focus. You may also modify the point of focus manually when recording, or afterward in the Photos app. Cinematic mode is accessible on every iPhone 14 model.

- Launch the camera, then pick the Cinematic mode.
- To zoom in before recording on an iPhone 14 Pro, or iPhone 14 Pro Max, press 3 next to 1x.

Before recording, press the Depth Adjustment button, then move the slider left or right to alter the depth-of-field effect.

- To begin recording, tap the Record button or touch either volume button.

A yellow frame denotes the person in focus, while a gray frame indicates that a human has been detected but is not in focus. Tap the gray box to change the focal point; tap again to fixate the focal point on that individual.

- To set the focal point if there is no person in the video, touch anywhere on the screen.
- To fix the focus on a single distance, touch and hold the screen.
- To stop recording, tap the Record button or hit either volume button.

On iPhone 14 models, you can modify the video resolution and frame rate using quick toggles at the top of the screen.

SHARE, VIEW, AND PRINT PHOTOS ON IPHONE

All images and movies captured using the Camera are stored in the Photos folder. When iCloud Photos is turned on, all new photos and videos are uploaded right away and can be seen in Photos on all devices with iCloud Photos (with iOS 8.1, iPadOS 13, or later).

Note: If Location Services is turned on in Settings > Privacy & Security > Location Services, images and videos are tagged with location information that apps and photo-sharing websites can use.

VIEW YOUR IMAGES

Tap the thumbnail picture in the lower-left area after launching the Camera.

- Swipe left or right to see your most recent images.
- Tap the display to reveal or conceal the controls.
- Tap All Photographs to see all of your Photos-stored photos and videos.

PRINT AND SHARE YOUR PHOTOGRAPHS

In the picture viewer, hit the Share button.

- Choose a way to share your pictures, such as AirDrop, Mail, or Messages.
- To print your shot, swipe up and choose Print from the list of things to do.

UPLOAD IMAGES AND MAINTAIN THEIR CONSISTENCY ACROSS DEVICES.

With iCloud Images, you can upload photos and videos from your iPhone to iCloud and then view them on other Apple-branded devices. iCloud Photos is helpful if you want to keep your photos up-to-date on multiple devices or save space on your iPhone. To turn on iCloud Photos, go to Settings > Photos.

USE LIVE TEXT WITH THE IPHONE CAMERA

On iPhone 14 pro, iPhone 14 pro max, and subsequent models, the Camera app may copy, share, look up, and translate text within the camera frame. Based on the text in the frame, the Camera also gives rapid actions to dial phone numbers, browse websites, convert currencies, and more.

Launch the Camera app, then position the iPhone so that the text shows inside the camera's frame.

After the yellow frame appears around identified text, hit the Live Text button and then do any of the below actions:

Copy Text: Copies text for pasting into a different application, such as Notes or Messages.

Choose All: Select the text contained inside the frame.

- Display customized online search results.
- The text must be translated.

Browse the web: Look up the highlighted text on the Internet.

Share: Share text through AirDrop, Messages, or Mail, among other possibilities.

You may also touch and hold the text, then use the grab points to pick a particular text and do the aforementioned operations.

Tap a fast action at the bottom of the screen to do actions like making a phone call, visiting a website, sending an email, and more.

To access the Camera, tap the Live Text On button.

To disable Live Text on the iPhone camera, go to Settings > Camera and disable Show Detected Text.

Made in the USA
Monee, IL
09 August 2024

63565887R00095